W9-CNI-772

THE NYACK LIBRARY
NYACK, N. Y. 10960

RUNNING BACKS

THE NYACK LIBRARY
NYACK, N. Y. 10960

Doug Marx

FOOTBALL
HEROES

The Rourke Corporation, Inc.
Vero Beach, Florida 32964

Copyright 1992 by The Rourke Corporation, Inc.

All rights reserved. No part of this book may be reproduced or utilized in any form or by any means, electronic or mechanical, including photocopying, recording or by any information storage and retrieval system without permission in writing from the publisher.

The Rourke Corporation, Inc.
P.O. Box 3328, Vero Beach, FL 32964

Marx, Doug.
        Running Backs / by Doug Marx.
                p. cm. — (Football heroes)
        Includes bibliographical references (p.47) and index.
        Summary: Discusses the basic strategy of the running game in football, the key positions involved, and some of the game's best players, including Jim Thorpe, O.J. Simpson, and Dave Meggett.
        ISBN 0-86593-151-8
                1. Backfield play (Football) — Juvenile literature. 2. Running backs (Football)—United States—Biography—Juvenile literature. [1. Backfield play (Football) 2. Football—History.] I.
Title. II. Series.
        GV951.3.M37 1992
        796.332'24—dc20   92-8764
                                                                                              CIP
                                                                                               AC

Series Editor: Gregory Lee
Editor: Marguerite Aronowitz
Book design and production: The Creative Spark, San Clemente, CA
Cover photograph: Rick Stewart/ALLSPORT

Contents

A Great Tradition   5

The Running Game   13

The Offensive Line   19

Halfbacks   25

Fullbacks And Tight Ends   33

Stats   44

Glossary   45

Bibliography   47

Index   48

The history of great running backs begins with Jim Thorpe, one of this century's greatest athletes.

A Great Tradition

Grace, agility, balance, speed, and instinct: five words that define the running back. For sheer excitement, not even the thrill of a long touchdown pass can measure up to the drama of a halfback breaking free of the pack and scampering 60 yards to the goal line. Or a fullback bursting up the middle, dragging two or three would-be tacklers along with him.

Quarterbacks might be football's glory boys. Wide receivers might be their pass-catching dance masters. But when it comes time to talk football and football heroes, the list of running backs can seem endless. Jim Thorpe, Harold "Red" Grange, Bronko Nagurski, Jim Brown, O.J. Simpson, Gale Sayers, Walter Payton, Eric Dickerson, Barry Sanders. There are 34

Running Back Trivia

Q: Who set a career record for two 90-yard touchdown runs?
A: Bo Jackson.

Q: What 1991 Hall of Fame member racked up four touchdowns against the Miami Dolphins to lead the Houston Oilers to a 35-30 victory in "The Greatest Monday Night Football Game"?
A: Earl Campbell.

Q: Who became the first player to gain 2,000 yards in a single NFL season?
A: O.J. Simpson.

running backs in the Hall of Fame, more than any other position.

Mention any one of these names to a football fan, and the forward pass is suddenly forgotten. The image that comes to mind is that of a lone ball carrier, pigskin tucked to his ribs, darting, leaping, sprinting, stiff-arming one would-be tackler, faking out another, racing downfield to the goal line. Nothing in football is more electrifying. From the New York Giants' "fly-boy" speedster Dave Meggett returning a punt 76 miraculous yards for a touchdown, to Christian Okoye barreling through a one-ton wall of defenders, this is the essence of football.

Running backs are the divers, survivors, and scrappers of the game. They take more punishment than any other player. Also, they are born, not taught, to run. They are made of reflexes and reactions. Their moves are spontaneous and free-flowing. True, a coach can teach a running back a team's playbook and how to make the most of his running talent, but after that he is on his own. It is said he runs for *daylight*.

In this book, we will take a look at football's great running backs of the past and present. We will examine each back position—halfback and fullback—as well as tight ends and kickoff-return specialists. The basic strategy of the running game will be discussed, together with a look at some of football's offensive setups, such as the "T" and "single-wing" formations. We will also consider the offensive front line: the guards and tackles who do the blocking, the nameless players without whom no running back can succeed.

The Early Days

When Barry Sanders of the Detroit Lions slices off-tackle, head-fakes a linebacker, stutter-steps a cornerback, and breaks toward the middle for a touchdown, that's a pure runner in action. Football is a brutal game that running backs like Sanders can turn into a ballet. Decked out in high-tech pads and shining helmets, their natural ability wears the disguise of a running machine.

It was not always this way. In 1870, 50 years before the National Football League (NFL) was formed, the first organized college football game was played between Rutgers and Princeton. Men had been playing soccer and rugby since the days of ancient Rome, and this first "football" game was a combination of those two sports. In fact, the rules stated that "no throwing or running" of the ball was allowed. The ball could only be batted, dribbled or kicked. Instead of touchdowns, a team scored one point for kicking the ball across the goal line. With 25 players on each side pushing, shoving, blocking, and ganging up on one another, scoring a goal was difficult.

As college teams practiced, the rugby style of play was preferred. These were bruising, bloody games. The players wore no protective equipment. By 1890, with the help and genius of star player Walter Camp, the foundation of today's game was set: one team got a series of four downs to gain 10 yards. A touchdown scored four points. Gone were the free-for-all riots of the game's beginnings. Camp's invention of the *scrimmage line* and *downs* created the need for offensive strategy. After a play had been called dead by an umpire, the offensive team could try another as long as they had downs remaining. Football came into its own as a distinctive American game, and the running game was born—sort of.

These were the days of the "flying wedge." The offensive blockers formed a "V" around the ball carrier, then charged into the defense. Although Amos Alonzo Stagg had by now invented the forward pass and the "T"

Harold "Red" Grange (right) was so fast that fans and foes alike called him "The Galloping Ghost."

formation, the game was still a pretty dull, grind-'em-out affair. Stagg modernized the game in other ways by inventing the place kick, the huddle, uniform numbers, the tackling dummy, the blocking sled, and goalpost pads.

By 1906, the forward pass was legalized in hopes of opening up the game and making it more exciting. But most teams did not use it more than three or four times per game.

Perhaps the greatest player of this era, the man

many call the greatest athlete in history, was Jim Thorpe. A Native American from the Sac and Fox tribe in Oklahoma, Thorpe won gold medals in the decathlon and pentathlon events in the 1912 Olympics. In 1913 he played professional baseball for the New York Giants. During his college days and later as a pro, he was a one-man offense on the football field who ran defenses ragged and drop kicked field goals to perfection—often scoring all of his team's points in a single game!

Unpadded and often unpaid, playing both offensively and defensively, players such as Thorpe were the heroes of early professional football. Then in 1922, the National Football League was formed. Much of the new league's success can be accounted for by the play of Harold "Red" Grange, a running back who attracted thousands of fans.

Also known as the "Galloping Ghost," Grange was the most highly publicized football player in history. In 20 varsity games for the University of Illinois, he scored 31 touchdowns and gained 3,637 yards. As a junior, he once scored five touchdowns against the University of Michigan, four of which came in the first 12 minutes of play!

These were heydays for runners. Backs like Thorpe and Grange were role models for today's players. Their blinding speed left would-be tacklers sprawled on the turf, clutching nothing but air. As the NFL became more popular and the passing game started to change the very nature of football itself, the rushing game took on more strategic importance.

In the post-World War II years, Jackie Robinson was breaking the color line in baseball (when only whites could compete against whites). In football, a future Hall of Fame fullback named Marion Motley was quietly doing the same, tearing up the gridiron for the Cleveland Browns. With coach Paul Brown at the helm

Bronko Nagurski was the Chicago Bears' big running star during the 1930s.

and quarterback Otto Graham running the offense (both future Hall of Famers), the Browns became the first modern NFL dynasty. And in Motley they had a running back (he also doubled as a linebacker) who many believed was the greatest all-around football player ever. To this day, Motley holds the career record for yards-per-carry with a 5.70 average!

Over the last 40 years, the passing game has become so crucial to football that it seems funny not to call it *arm*ball. Let's not forget that without a solid ground attack a passing game is useless. Even when it seems that some teams do nothing but pass, pass, pass, the statistical truth is that the ball is generally on the ground at least 50 percent of the time. It was not until the mid-1980s that a few teams had winning seasons by throwing the ball more than they ran it.

Football is still very much a runner's game. As we move into the 1990s, running backs are ready to take their place in the Hall of Fame tradition. With ground gainers such as Detroit's Barry Sanders, the Chiefs' Christian Okoye, Buffalo's Thurman Thomas, and the Vikings' Roger Craig chewing up the yardage, there is no chance the running game will become obsolete.

THE NYACK LIBRARY
NYACK. N. Y. 10960

Marcus Allen has run plenty of off-tackle slants and sweeps in gaining more than 8,000 yards in his career.

The Running Game

As we have seen, in the old days the running game was the only game. Whether slogging it out behind the flying wedge, or breaking free with running displays like Thorpe and Grange, running backs were football's heroes.

By the 1950s, the so-called "Golden Age of Pro Football," quarterbacks emerged as the new stars. The basic offensive strategy—which would last for another 25 years—called for a steady, no-nonsense ground attack to set up the defense, then throw a quick pass that would catch them leaning. The majority of touchdowns might come as a result of the pass, but the running game still carried most of the offensive responsibility.

The dawn of the passing game had the effect of changing the defensive game. Teams were soon moving defenders from the front line into the backfield, creating new positions such as middle linebacker. The *T-formation* had been the offensive standard for many years, especially as the passing game evolved. But as defenses changed to counter the pass, offensive setups also changed in turn.

Vince Lombardi, the coach of the 1960s' tough Green Bay Packers, scrapped the T and went back to the old single wing style. Lombardi brought back the running game. His favorite play was called the *sweep*. Using two guards, a tight end and a fullback as blockers, Lombardi devised an unstoppable running attack led by fullback Jim Taylor and halfback Paul Hornung. "Setting up the pass with the run," became the Lombardi strategy. With Bart Starr at quarterback throwing touchdown bombs to ends Max McGee and Boyd Dowler, the Packers won six NFL Championships —not to mention Super Bowls I and II!

Although the Packer dynasty could not last forever, the Lombardi strategy proved more durable. In the 1970s, as the NFL and AFL merged into the huge National Football League of today, most successful teams still ran the ball about 60 percent of the time but scored touchdowns on passes about 60 percent of the time. Again, the run set up the pass. This logic still holds true today.

The running game can be divided into two parts: The *inside* and the *outside* game. The inside running game means power and control. It is the blood-and-guts game, directed up the middle between the defensive guards. First downs come hard, yard by yard. Generally, the inside game is the domain of fullbacks.

There are other, more strategic reasons for running inside. For example, working a quick count, a quarterback might send a running back up the middle on a "quick hit," just to keep the defense honest. As the defense bunches up to protect against the quick hit, the quarterback can then resort to the pass.

The outside running game calls for the two most basic rushing plays in football: the *off-tackle slant* and the sweep. Running off-tackle, a back charges just outside the defensive tackle. This is one of pro football's bread-and-butter plays, because it hits the weakest point of the defensive line. If a team can use the off-tackle slant with success, the defense will have to weaken itself in order to compensate.

The sweep, which brought Vince Lombardi's Packers so much success, simply takes the slant farther outside. The ball carrier runs around the defensive end.

*The NFL's Offensive Rookie of the Year (1990) was the busy
Emmitt Smith, who was fifth in rushing touchdowns.*

To be successful, a sweep requires guards who are fast
enough to pull from their front line positions and lead
the blocking charge. The running back must be fast
enough to turn that outside corner and head upfield
before the linebackers can get to him.

There are a number of sweep plays, and a good
running back needs to know how to follow his blockers.
On a *power sweep*, the two pulling guards lead a
halfback. On a *fullback sweep*, the halfback leads the
blocking charge. With the *option sweep*, the ball carrier
might choose to pass if he can find an open receiver.

Putting a *man in motion* means that a running
back takes one step forward and jogs parallel to the
scrimmage line before the ball is snapped. This puts him

Ottis Anderson's running for the Giants earned him the MVP award in Super Bowl XXV.

closer to the outside, where he might take a quick pitch-out or flare pass, or serve as a lead blocker. Sometimes the man in motion is a receiver who becomes a potential ball carrier or lead blocker. Mostly, however, the man in motion is designed to confuse the defense. This is especially true if the defense is playing man-to-man.

All offenses have trick plays. The *reverse* is probably the best-known trick play. On a reverse, the quarterback charges in one direction, and then hands off to a back running the other way. On a double reverse, the running back hands the ball off *again* to an end or another back charging in the quarterback's original direction. Gadget plays like this are dangerous and used sparingly because the action takes place far behind the line of scrimmage. If the defense reads them correctly, a team can be thrown for a big loss. Also, the trickier the play, the greater the chance of a fumble or mental mistake.

The *Ace* or one-back formation is one of the new offensive trends of the 1990s. It is a strong and powerful formation best used by a team with a superior running back. In the Ace formation, one lone running back stands fairly deep in the backfield right behind the quarterback. The other running back, called an *up back*, is usually in motion—moving up and out of the backfield—to be used as a blocker or extra receiver. This puts a lot of pressure on the defense, from the scrimmage line to the goal line. With so many potential pass catchers, the defense must give top priority to its pass rush, which is the opening the one-back needs for a big gain on the ground.

No matter how much football strategy turns to the pass, the running game will always be a vital part of offensive strategy. Over the years coaches have invented new backfield formations. From the single wing to the one-back setup, coaches are looking for new ways to confuse the defense. Who knows what kind of offensive setups will be employed in the future?

No running back could succeed without the blocking power of tackles like 10-time Pro Bowler Anthony Munoz.

The Offensive Line

No look at running backs would be complete without some discussion of the offensive line. The offensive line is where the game begins. Running backs know this better than anyone. When O.J. Simpson broke Jim Brown's single-season NFL record for yards gained with 2,003 in 1973, he invited his offensive linemen to the postgame celebration. After the 1977 NFL season when Walter Payton led the league in rushing, he said thank you to his linemen by giving them watches. And when Tony Dorsett was named a Dallas Cowboy player of the week, winning several pairs of cowboy boots, he gave them to—guess who?—his offensive linemen.

Except to their backfield mates, offensive linemen are the anonymous heroes of football. The work of offensive linemen is not covered by statistics. You will not find their heroics numbered in the record books. It is impossible to do, so they remain nameless.

And what heroics make the offensive line so important? They block. They block for the runner, and they block for the passer. When it comes to blocking, they are the experts. There are angle blocks, wedges, double teams, and cross blocks. An offensive lineman has to be quick enough to pull out of position at the snap and lead the sweep. He has to be strong enough to hold back the defensive line tidal wave on a pass rush. Without guard Forrest Gregg and tackle Fuzzy

Thurston, Vince Lombardi's championship Packer teams of the 1960s might have been also-rans.

Today, offensive linemen still remain anonymous, best known for what does *not* happen when they are on the field. Take sacks, for example. Two of the game's best tandem guards, the Oilers' Mike Munchak and Bruce Matthews, led an offensive line in 1989 that went six games without having a sack scored against it. Not once was their quarterback tackled behind the line of scrimmage. That is not a statistic you will find in the record books, but it is one that Warren Moon, the Oiler quarterback, remembers well.

Although age and injuries are starting to catch up with him, Cincinnati tackle Anthony Munoz is regarded as the blocker of the 1980s, if not the best tackle of all time. A ten-time Pro Bowler, Munoz is murder on pass rushers, and more than one defender has had a slow time getting up after one of his blocks.

Then there is the center. More than just the guy who snaps the ball, the center is crucial to the offensive line. He is sometimes called the "other quarterback." The center makes calls on the line that help his teammates cope with shifting defenses. He is the man who reads the defense and tells his fellow linemen how to block: straight ahead, or at an angle.

In the running game, a team will usually rush toward their *strong side*, which is the side on which the tight end lines up. Tight ends, besides protecting the quarterback on pass rushes, are the key blockers on sweeps. This extra strength on the line lets a team use its quicker, lighter running backs. Running to the *weak side*, on the other hand, calls for a bigger, stronger runner, someone who can run over would-be tacklers.

One of the game's recent trends is the *unbalanced line*. In this setup, another lineman, usually a tackle, is shifted to the strong side. This formation allows for a

All-time leading rusher Walter Payton never would have reached his 16,726 yards without a solid offensive line.

A running back like Roger Craig has to be able to read the defense, and the blocks of his teammates, to gain crucial yardage.

much more powerful strong side running attack, but it also leaves the weak side back door open for charging defenders to drop a ball carrier or passer for a loss.

Draw and *trap* running plays are specialties of the offensive line. On draw plays, when the ball is snapped, the offensive line pretends to block as if the play were a pass. They might stutter-step in place, or back up a bit as if to encircle and protect the quarterback. The running backs also take up pass blocking positions. Then, at the last second, with the defense fooled and charging the quarterback, the ball is handed to a back who bolts right up the middle for daylight. If the offensive line is not convincing in its fake, the defense will hold its ground and swallow up the runner.

The trap play also involves deceptive movement by the offensive linemen. In this case, the lineman at the point of attack pulls away at the snap, leaving an apparent hole for the defender to charge through. But then that defender is immediately blocked by a lineman pulling from the other side of the line! Thus, if a right guard pulls, blocking to his right as the defensive tackle barrels through—surprise!—he is blocked by the left tackle, who has also pulled right.

Tackle and center traps, short and long traps, sucker traps—all are part of the offensive line's strategy. Used well, these blocking patterns can confuse a defense and make it vulnerable to head-on attacks. Offensive linemen often think of themselves as technical, rather than instinctive players. They need more control than defensive players, and tend to be less emotional than their defensive counterparts. Plus all that, they must be good actors. Without them, not even O.J. Simpson could get beyond the line of scrimmage.

*Tony Dorsett was the Cowboys' dependable running back for years,
second on the all-time rushing list with 12,739 yards.*

Halfbacks

When we think of clever, fleet-footed running backs, we think of halfbacks. These are the guys who can give a head-fake to the right and dart 90 degrees to the left at top speed without losing a step.

Because of the variety of offensive setups used in today's game, the backfield no longer consists of two halfbacks and a fullback. Some backs are called wingbacks, others tailbacks. Still others move out to a position called flanker, where they become a pass receiver. Given this confusion, "running back" is the term most often used to generally describe the halfback and fullback positions.

Among the all-time Hall of Fame halfback greats of the past are such players as Baltimore's Lenny Moore, the 49ers' Hugh McElhenney, and Ollie Matson, who played for both the Cardinals and the Rams. These rushers set the style in the football boom years of the 1950s and early 1960s. Then there is the Bears' legendary Gale Sayers, whose career was cut short in 1968 by a knee injury. He was only 25, just coming into his prime.

Looking back on Sayers' career, fans and sportswriters point to his league-leading stats as evidence of his Hall of Fame standing. Imagine: Sayers was elected to the Hall of Fame on the strength of three good years! In 1965, his rookie season, he scored six touchdowns in one game!—four on runs, one on a pass, and another on a punt return. That same year he set an

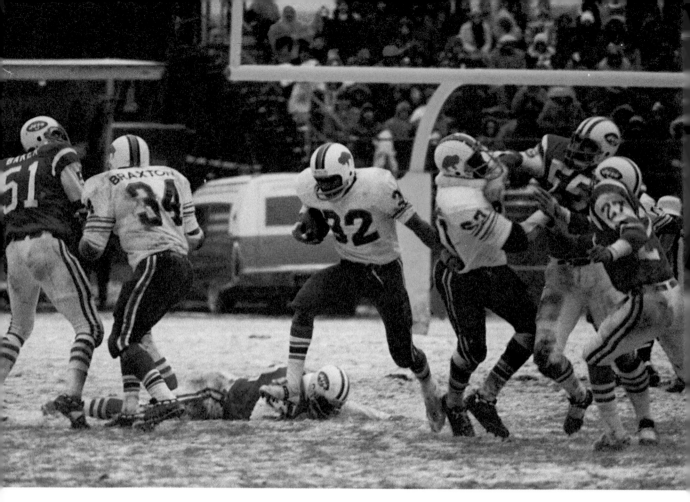

In 1969 the Buffalo Bills drafted USC's O.J. Simpson, one of the most exciting running backs of the 1970s. "The Juice" was the first player to rush for more than 2,000 yards in a single season.

NFL record, scoring 22 touchdowns. Amazingly, he only got better, until he was injured.

Putting records aside, however, Sayers' real achievement was to define a new kind of halfback. Prior to his appearance in the game, halfbacks were small, weighing 175-185 pounds, and not known for their power. Sayers changed all that. He was like a combination halfback and fullback. He could break through the middle like a bull and, finding daylight, race through the open field like a deer.

As it happened, just about the time Sayers' playing days were ending, another halfback appeared on the scene to carry the day, and the new decade: Orenthal

James Simpson. "O.J." for short. At six-feet, two-inches and 215 pounds, Simpson ran defenses dizzy with a combination of speed, deception, and power that made him one of the game's best two or three running backs.

Incredibly, Simpson's record-breaking seasons came while playing for the Buffalo Bills, a team that never made it to the Super Bowl during his entire career. Entering the pros in 1969 after his Heisman Trophy days with the USC Trojans, Simpson got off to a slow start. Then, in 1973, he broke free. He opened the year with a 250-yard day against the Patriots, and ended it with a 200-yard game against the Jets. Along the way, he broke almost every single-season rushing record on the books, finishing with 2,003 yards. That accomplishment broke Jim Brown's 1963 record of 1,863 yards. It would be another 11 years before the Colts' Eric Dickerson would finally top Simpson with a 2,105-yard season.

Simpson earned several single-season rushing titles, not to mention a number of single-game records. In 1977, Simpson became the second running back in history to rack up more than 10,000 yards. Again, Jim Brown's lifetime record of 12,312 yards was on the line, but injuries and a weak Buffalo line held Simpson's lifetime mark to 11,236 yards. He retired in 1979.

Through the late '70s and '80s, other running backs would soon topple Jim Brown's and O.J. Simpson's records. Playing for the Super Bowl-winning Cowboys, Tony Dorsett gained a lifetime 12,739 yards. A fan would think a running back could do no more, but during the same time that Dorsett and the Cowboys were having championship years, the Bears' Walter Payton was setting even higher standards.

During his 1975 to 1987 pro career, Payton did it all. Today, he holds lifetime records in attempts, with 3,838; yards gained, with 16,726; and touchdowns, with

110! Those 16,726 yards gained are 4,000 more than his closest rival, Tony Dorsett. Like Simpson, Payton played on Bears teams that did not do well in post-season play. He did make it to the Super Bowl, however, and Payton now has a Super Bowl ring.

These all-stars were in a league of their own. They had all the skills: quickness of *lateral* (or left/right) motion, speed, balance and agility. They were born runners. They were all instinct and nerve. Running backs have to be smart, and they have to be able to learn complex offensive playbooks. Still, no one can teach them how to run—that comes naturally. That is why so many rookies come into the game and set the turf on fire.

Of equal importance, running backs do a lot more than just score touchdowns: they must also block. They must sacrifice themselves. If a running back blocks well for his teammates, team morale goes up because the other players know he is not a "prima donna." Knowing this, they will block well for him when it is his turn to run with the ball. Also, running backs must know how to go into a play empty-handed, faking it. Between blocking assignments, getting hit on fakes, and getting hit on carries, running backs take as much or more punishment than any other position.

Among the running backs of the 1990s, several are lining up to challenge the greatness of Sayers, Simpson, and Payton. An NFC Rookie of the Year and first-team All-Pro in 1989, Detroit's Barry Sanders is greased lightning. A solid pass blocker and sure-handed receiver, at five-feet, six-inches and 200 pounds he is untouchable. Sanders is a touchdown threat any time he gets his hands on the ball. His specialty is the 15- or 20-yard gain on a draw play when it is third down and long yardage.

On the basis of his first two pro seasons, Sanders

Detroit's Barry Sanders is the new kid on the block, helping his team make the 1991 NFL playoffs.

is thought of by sportswriters and coaches as the best running back in football. The Bills' Thurman Thomas and the Bears' Neal Anderson are his equals. A fast, heavy-duty runner who packs the pigskin upward of 18 times a game, Thomas gained a league-leading 1,829 yards in 1990 for the Buffalo Bills. Over 500 of those yards came on 49 pass receptions, which makes Thomas a double threat. His 190 yards and a 31-yard touchdown run against New York in Super Bowl XXV were enough to make him Buffalo's MVP in their losing effort to the Giants.

Neal Anderson is considered the league's most versatile running back. Joining the Bears in 1986, he has become the heir to Walter Payton's great career. All

A running back who routinely runs 1,000 yards each season is Chicago's Neal Anderson, who is also a mean pass receiver.

that Sanders has on him is youth. With more moves than a mongoose, great vision and power like a freight train, Anderson is unstoppable. He is also a ferocious, bone-crunching blocker.

There are so many good halfbacks on the field today that to single out Sanders, Thomas, and Anderson seems unfair. For example, four-time Pro Bowler James Brooks of the Browns averages five-plus yards per carry and catches everything thrown his way. In 1991, former 49er Pro Bowler and Super Bowl hero Roger Craig moved to the Raiders, where he teamed up with veteran halfback Marcus Allen (another in a long line of great running backs out of USC).

Allen is thought of as the ultimate "money back." When the big game is on the line, Allen comes through. His 1983 post-season performance may never be equaled: 121 yards versus the Steelers, 154 yards versus the Seahawks, and 191 yards in the Raiders' 38-9 Super Bowl rout of the Redskins. In 1990, a bit past his prime, Allen literally carried the Raiders after Bo Jackson had to leave the field—and the sport—forever. Bo Jackson was the only running back in football history to have two 90-yard-plus scoring runs. Jackson might have left everyone in the dust if his career had not been cut so short.

From Jim Thorpe to Red Grange to O.J. Simpson to Barry Sanders, these are but a few of the players who have made halfback the game's spectacular point of action. Requiring running, blocking, receiving, and passing skills, it is football's all-around position.

THE NYACK LIBRARY
NYACK, N. Y. 10960

The mighty Pittsburgh Steelers, who won four Super Bowls in the 1970s, had Franco Harris on their side.

Fullbacks And Tight Ends

Fullbacks define the bone-crunching running game. They are the big backs with quick feet who can head-butt a defensive wall and pick up a couple of yards. In the old days they had names such as Cliff Battles and Ken Strong, names that reflected their toughness. Others were given nicknames. Alphonse Leemans was known as "Tuffy." Then there was Clarence "Pug" Manders, who in 1941 led the NFL in rushing with a whopping 486 yards! Paul Younger was called "Tank."

Then there was Hall of Famer Bronko Nagurski, who played in the mud and snow for the Chicago Bears through the 1930s. He was the finest fullback of his era, a massive ground-gainer who could knock down trees. When the Hall of Fame was born in 1963, Nagurski was one of the first elected, right up there with

Running Back Trivia

Q: Name the running back who, in 1975, led the NFL in rushing and scoring.
A: O.J. Simpson. That year he outrushed nine NFL teams, set a single-season touchdown record with 23, and became the second player in NFL history to score a TD in every game.

Q: Who holds the NFL single-season record for rushing?
A: Eric Dickerson, with 2,105 yards.

Q: What player holds the single-season record for touchdowns?
A: John Riggins, with 24.

The greatest running back of all time? Most fans will still say Jim Brown. His awesome power helped him average more than 100 yards per game.

Jim Thorpe and "Red" Grange.

When football talk comes around to running backs, a fan will hear several names tossed out as "the greatest ever." We have already discussed the likes of O.J. Simpson, Gale Sayers and Walter Payton. But the one player all of these running backs looked up to as their model of greatness was fullback Jim Brown. Although many of his records have long since been broken, Brown remains the standard that all ball carriers admire.

Brown changed the position and the game. He was

six-foot, two-inches, and 228 pounds. In his nine-year career with the Cleveland Browns he averaged more than 100 yards per game, not to mention 5.22 yards per carry—second only to Marion Motley on the lifetime leaders list. Mixing brute power, blazing speed, and darting moves like a bat in flight, Brown was almost impossible to bring down. New York Giant middle linebacker Sam Huff once said of Brown: "All you can do is grab him, hold on, and wait for help."

In the decade before Brown's arrival, Hall of Famer Joe Perry started the tradition of the fleet-footed fullback. In 1947, he ran the 100-yard dash in 9.5 seconds! During 16 rugged seasons through the 1950s, playing mostly with the 49ers, Perry averaged 5.04 yards per carry, picked up 9,723 yards, and scored 71 touchdowns. Those are very big numbers for a running back of that era. Back then, 12 rather than 16 games made a season, and running backs did not carry the ball as much. Jim Brown, for example, had two-to-three hundred attempts per season. Joe Perry would have one-to-two hundred. As if these obstacles were not enough, Perry also had to contend with racism. Together with Marion Motley, he helped break the "color line" in pro football.

In the years since Brown's retirement in 1965, some amazing fullbacks have dominated the game. The 1970s were owned by Franco Harris of the Steelers and Larry Csonka of the Dolphins. Harris continued the speedster tradition, and "Big Zonk"—weighing 240 pounds—simply ran over the opposition.

Harris held the fullback slot for the Steelers through 12 seasons, a career that included four Super Bowl championships. As a pass catcher, a kickoff-return specialist, and a rusher, he racked up 16,700 yards in regular and post-season play. At six-feet, two-inches, and 225 pounds, Harris ran with what is called a

What weights 260 pounds and travels 40 yards in under five seconds? It's Kansas City's Christian Okoye.

"tiptoe" style. He darted and dodged around defenders rather than barreling into them.

"Big Zonk" preferred to knock them down. In 1972, gaining 1,117 yards in regular season play, he led the Dolphins to a Super Bowl championship and the only perfect season in NFL history (17-0). Talking about the art of running the football, Csonka once said: "Running backs have to be big and strong, but they also have to enjoy the chase, like kids do. If you were a kid who loved to have people chase you, you've got the beginnings of a running back."

Through the 1980s, Eric Dickerson of the Rams and the Colts has been rewriting the record books. From 1983 to 1989, Dickerson set an NFL record with seven consecutive 1,000-yard seasons! O.J. Simpson once called Dickerson "the best I've ever seen, and I mean ever."

A couple of younger fullbacks are currently making names for themselves. John L. Williams of Seattle is a dependable all-round fullback. He contributes on several levels. In 1990 he caught 70 passes and picked up over 700 yards on the ground. Williams is like a tight end, a speedy halfback, and a blocking guard all rolled into one.

At 248 pounds, Marion Butts holds down the "singleback" slot in San Diego's Ace formation. He hits the line like a cannon ball and punishes the defense with his blocks. Able to break gang-tackles, in 1990 Butts rushed for 1,225 yards and averaged 4.6 yards per carry.

Another big, strong fullback is Chicago's Brad Muster. Some observers feel he is the perfect complement to Bears' halfback Neal Anderson. Like Butts, Muster is a tough, selfless fullback with multiple skills. These two running backs might not ever lead the league in rushing stats, but their reliable play might well lead their teams to winning seasons.

Just as Barry Sanders is being called the halfback

of the 1990s, Christian Okoye is being touted as the decade's fullback. Okoye is a 260-pound track star from Nigeria who runs the 40-yard dash in 4.46 seconds. He has only been playing football since 1985, when he tried out for the Azusa Pacific college team. Okoye led the NFL in rushing in his rookie year with 1,480 yards.

Still learning, this mammoth fullback has a tendency to fumble. He also needs to improve his ability to follow blockers. In his 1990 sophomore year, his stats dropped considerably because of his inexperience. Even so, he can bulldoze the defense or outrun it. Born in 1961 and getting a late career start, Okoye will probably not have a long future in football. Nevertheless, many expect he will dominate the game for as long as he can.

Tight Ends

Although not strictly running backs, tight ends are very much a part of any team's rushing game. The tight end must know how to block as well as offensive guards and tackles. He must also have the quickness to run pass patterns, and sticky fingers to make receptions. Tight ends are the supermen of football: Tall and tough, lean and mean, fast as speeding bullets.

The jobs of the tight end are many. Tight end is the only position in football that started in the pros, rather than college play. In the 1930s, coaches started bringing one of their wide receivers in close to a tackle, giving additional blocking strength. But it was not until the late 1950s that Ron Kramer perfected this play, becoming the first modern tight end.

Kramer was a part of the Green Bay Packer dynasty coached by Vince Lombardi. As a blocker, Kramer led the famous sweep that destroyed Packer opponents. Then, when defenses started keying on the sweep, Kramer would run a pass pattern and come up with a touchdown reception. In 1962, a championship year for the Packers, Kramer caught 37 passes for 555 yards and seven TDs.

Retiring from the game in 1967, Kramer set the standard for tight ends of the future. John Mackey of the Colts proved that a tight end could be as hard to bring down as a running back. A five-time Pro Bowler, in 1966 Mackey caught 50 passes, gained 829 yards, and crossed the goal line nine times. Other big-name tight ends of the 1970s and 1980s include the Lions' Charlie Sanders, the Raiders' Dave Casper, and the Browns' Ozzie Newsome. And last but not least, there is Mike Ditka, who played for the Bears and now coaches them—the only tight end in the Hall of Fame.

Today, tight end is a position so important that some teams will build their entire offense around a good one. A tight end who can run, block, and catch passes keeps a defense worried and honest. Redskins veteran Don Warren, for example, was a key element in Washington's running game through the 1980s.

The Eagles' Keith Byars is another tight end cut from this pattern. He is listed as a "running back" on the team roster, although he lines up as fullback, halfback, tight end, and wide receiver in a variety of setups. In 1990 he had 37 rushing attempts as a running back, which is quite low—but he led all NFL runners with 81 receptions and 819 yards through the air! Now, that kind of "what-is-he-going-to-do-next" player will give a defense fits.

Cincinnati's Rodney Holman is widely considered the best blocking tight end in the business. Holman is the kind of tight end who figures that a key block that helps his halfback gain 20 yards is equal to a 20-yard pass reception. He is selfless, a team player. In spite of his value as a blocker, he caught 40 passes in 1990, averaging over 14 yards per catch.

And finally, there is the Eagles' Keith Jackson. A

The best punt and kickoff return specialists, players like Dave Meggett, dash into the jaws of the opposition—and love it.

starter in the Pro Bowl through his first three seasons, Jackson caught a total 194 passes—tops in the league. He was the NFC Rookie of the Year in 1988 with 81 receptions! Besides solid blocking ability, Jackson is thought of as the best third-down receiver in the game, which is a crucial responsibility. If he is lucky and stays healthy, Jackson could someday make people forget about past stars like Kramer and Ditka.

Special Teams

Years ago, special teams were often called "suicide squads." Today, although special teams is the familiar term used for these offensive and defensive units, coaches still often refer to their special-team players as "maniacs" and "fanatics."

No wonder. Imagine that you are New York Giants running back Dave Meggett. You are five-foot, seven-inches, and 180 pounds. Several times in each game you stand all alone at the far end of the field, waiting for a high punt or kickoff to come down out of the sky and into your arms. Waiting for it to drop, you hear what sounds like a cattle stampede charging right at you. It is your job not only to catch the ball, but to run it back right through that stampede. It could be the most dangerous play in pro football. And the most exciting.

Meggett does this game after game for the Giants. In 1990, he led the Super Bowl-winning Giants with 1,533 "all-purpose" yards. Nearly 1,000 of those yards were gained on kickoff and punt returns. Kickers are so spooked by Meggett that they try to kick the ball some place where he cannot catch it.

Meggett is a rare breed in that not many running backs double as return specialists. Most coaches are unwilling to risk injury to their star running backs. Consequently, many of the game's superior runners, the return artists, do not get much attention—except when they break loose for a 70- or 80-yard run.

Mel Gray, for example, is listed as a wide receiver, but it is as a kickoff specialist that he has proven himself. In 1990 for the Detroit Lions Gray led all comers with a kickoff-return average of 22.9 yards and a punt-return average of 10.6 yards. These stats earned him his first Pro Bowl berth.

Also in 1990 cornerback "Neon" Deion Sanders led the Atlanta Falcons with 1,254 total yards! With 851 yards in kickoff returns, another 250 in punts, and 153 in pass interceptions, Sanders gained more ground than his team's running backs! Not bad for a defensive player.

Special teams have become a crucial aspect of pro football. The level of competition is so equal in the pros that success at the kicking, coverage, and return games is all-important to championship play. Special teams have an influence on the game far out of proportion to the time they spend on the field. It should not be surprising to learn that teams that make the playoffs always have solid, league-leading special teams.

With respect to kickoff-return specialists, there is a lot more to their position than the thrills and spills of a long touchdown run. For example, as simple as it might sound, the most important skill for a return man is catching the football—every time. When it comes to kicking plays, there is no room for fumbles, not even one. It's not easy to catch a punt or kickoff, and a fumble can be costly. A smart coach would rather have an average runner who never fumbles than a spectacular runner who has occasional butterfingers.

Punt returns also call for lightning-quick decision making. The receiver must choose whether to run the ball, call a "fair catch," or let the ball bounce until it is downed or called dead by the umpire. Again, with more than a ton of defensive flesh bearing down hard on the receiver, this is not a snap decision. Similarly, a kickoff-return man must often choose whether to attempt a runback from his own end zone, or accept a touchback and let his team take over on their 20-yard line. Given that punt and kickoff receivers might have as many as 50 or 60 plays each in the course of a season, it is easy to see how important their play is to a team.

Most teams specialize their punt and kickoff men, as well. Dave Meggett is unusual in that he plays both positions. Generally, a punt-return man is swivel-hipped and sure-footed, an open-field runner, while a kickoff-return man is a pure sprinter. The main goal of a punt returner is to regain decent field position for the offensive squad. Although a good number of single-season punt-return record holders have averaged as much as 20 yards per carry, half that number is considered excellent work. Among modern players, no punt-return artist has a lifetime average higher than 12-plus yards.

A kickoff-return specialist, catching the ball near or in the end zone, races upfield trying to get to the 20-yard line or beyond. Anything more than that is considered icing on the cake. In his short career with the Bears, Gale Sayers averaged 37.7 yards on kickoff returns during the 1967 season. That same year, Green Bay's Travis Williams turned in a 41.1 average! Sayers leads the lifetime kickoff return average with 30.6 yards per carry.

Special-team running backs might be football's most spectacular players. Whether settling under a kickoff or a high, spiraling punt, they have the attention of everyone in the stadium. The crowd holds its breath, the defenders charge, the ball seems to take forever to come down, and then, grace, speed, agility, balance, and instinct take over as the man with the ball looks for daylight and a touchdown.

All-Time NFL Rushing Leaders

	Carries	Yards	Avg.	TD
Walter Payton	3,838	16,726	4.4	110
Tony Dorsett	2,936	12,739	4.3	77
Jim Brown	2,359	12,312	5.2	106
Franco Harris	2,949	12,120	4.1	91
Eric Dickerson*	2,616	11,903	4.6	86
John Riggins	2,916	11,352	3.9	104
O.J. Simpson	2,404	11,236	4.7	61
Ottis Anderson*	2,499	10,101	4.0	80
Earl Campbell	2,187	9,407	4.3	74
Jim Taylor	1,941	8,597	4.4	83
Joe Perry	1,737	8,378	4.8	53
Larry Csonka	1,891	8,081	4.3	64
Marcus Allen*	1,960	7,957	4.1	75
Gerald Riggs*	1,911	7,940	4.2	58
Freeman McNeil*	1,704	7,604	4.5	36

*Players still active.

Glossary

ACE FORMATION. Also called the *one-back formation*, this is an offensive setup that leaves only a single rusher behind the quarterback while the other back (the *up back*) is in motion.

CUTBACK. The movement when a ball carrier changes direction and runs against the flow of the play.

DAYLIGHT. Any opening or hole in the defense through which a ball carrier might run.

DRAW PLAY. When the offensive line blocks to make the defense think a pass is coming. They "draw" the defense around to the outside until the running back threads through the middle.

DOWN. A play from scrimmage. Each team gets four downs—first through fourth—in which to make ten yards.

FAIR CATCH. A catch by the receiver of a punt or kickoff when he cannot be touched or tackled by the defense. To signal a fair catch, the runner raises one arm over his head. Once the signal is made he cannot run with the ball, and the defense will be penalized if he is touched.

FLANKER. The wide receiver on the tight end's side (strong side) of the offensive formation. The flanker is officially a member of the backfield, and must set up one yard behind the scrimmage line.

HOLE. The gap that blockers open for a runner.

LEAD BLOCK. A block thrown by one running back leading another running back into the defensive line.

MAN IN MOTION. When one running back gparallel to the line of scrimmage, before the ball is snapped, to confuse the defense.

OFF-TACKLE SLANT. When a running back charges outside the defensive tackle.

PULL. When an offensive lineman, usually a guard or tackle, leaves his position at the snap of the ball to lead a running play.

REVERSE. A running play that changes direction in the backfield once, sometimes twice.

SCRIMMAGE LINE. The yard line where the football is placed after each down to begin the next play.

STRONG SIDE. The side of the offensive line with the tight end.

SWEEP. A slant play that runs outside the defensive end. There is the *power sweep* led by two guards, a *fullback sweep*, and the *option sweep*, when the ball carrier can pass if he finds an open receiver.

T-FORMATION. Three backs and the quarterback line up behind the center in what looks like the letter "T."

TOUCHBACK. When the football is whistled dead behind a team's goal line. One example occurs when a kickoff goes into the end zone and the receiver signals "fair catch." The ball is then placed on the 20-yard line.

TRAP PLAY. When a lineman pulls off the line of scrimmage after the ball is snapped, letting a defender through until he is blocked by a different lineman.

UNBALANCED LINE. When both tackles line up on the strong side of the center.

WEAK SIDE. The side of the offensive line with the wide end.

Picture Credits

ALLSPORT USA: 12 (Stephen Dunn); 15 (Doug Pensinger); 16 (Otto Greule); 18, 29 (Rick Stewart); 21 (Mike Powell); 22 (Ken Levine); 24 (J. Rettaliata); 30 (J. Daniel); 32 (Bob Grieser); 36 (Tim DeFrisco); 40 (Commentucci)

NFL Properties: 4, 8

Wide World Photos: 10, 26, 34

Bibliography

Books

Anderson, Dave. *The Story of Football*. New York: William Morrow, 1985

Barron, Bill, Larry Eldridge, Jr., Chuck Garrity, Jr., Jim Natal, and Beau Riffenburgh. *The Illustrated NFL Playbook*. New York: Workman Publishing, 1988.

Carroll, Bob, Pete Palmer, and John Thorn. *The Hidden Game of Football*. New York: Warner Books, 1988.

Cohen, Richard M., and David S. Neft. *The Sports Encyclopedia: Pro Football*. New York: St. Martin's Press, 1991.

Hollander, Zander. *1991 Complete Handbook of Pro Football*. New York: Signet, 1991.

Lamb, Kevin. *Quarterbacks, Nickelbacks, and Other Loose Change*. Chicago: Contemporary Books, 1984.

Wilkinson, Bud. *Sports Illustrated Football: Offense*. New York: J.B. Lippincott Company, 1972.

Zimmerman, Paul. *A Thinking Man's Guide to Pro Football*. New York: E.P. Dutton, 1971.

Periodicals

Lamb, Kevin, and Chris Mortensen. "The NFL's Best." *Sport*, October 1991: 40.

Miller, J. David. "The NFL's Super 78." *Sport*, August 1990: 37.

Index

Allen, Marcus, 12, 31
Anderson, Neal, 29-31, 37
Anderson, Ottis, 16

Battles, Cliff, 33
Brooks, James, 31
Brown, Jim, 5, 19, 27, 34-35
Butts, Marion, 37
Byars, Keith, 39

Camp, Walter, 7
Campbell, Earl, 5
Casper, Dave, 39
Craig, Roger, 11, 22, 31
Csonka, Larry, 35-37

Dickerson, Eric, 5, 27, 33, 37
Ditka, Mike, 39, 40
Dorsett, Tony, 19, 24, 27, 28

fullbacks, 33-38

Grange, Harold "Red," 5, 8, 9, 13, 31, 34
Gray, Mel, 42
Gregg, Forrest, 19

halfbacks, 25-31
Harris, Franco, 32, 35
Holman, Rodney, 39
Hornung, Paul, 14

Jackson, Bo, 5, 31
Jackson, Keith, 39-40

Kramer, Ron, 38-39, 40

Leemans, Alphonse, 33
Lombardi, Vince, 13-14, 20, 38

Mackey, John, 39
Manders, Clarence "Pug," 33
Matson, Ollie, 25
Matthews, Bruce, 20
McElhenney, Hugh, 25
Meggett, Dave, 6, 40-41, 43
Moore, Lenny, 25
Motley, Marion, 9-11, 35
Munchak, Mike, 20
Munoz, Anthony, 18, 20

Nagurski, Bronko, 5, 10, 33
National Football League (NFL), 7, 9
Newsome, Ozzie, 39

offensive line, 19-23
Okoye, Christian, 6, 11, 36, 38

Payton, Walter, 5, 19, 21, 27-28, 29, 34
Perry, Joe, 35

Riggins, John, 33
running backs
    and blocking, 28
    and the running game, 13-17
    in the Hall of Fame, 5-6
    rushing leaders, 44
running plays
    and formations, 17, 20-21
    draw, 23
    man in motion, 15
    off-tackle slant, 14
    reverse, 17
    sweep, 13-14
    trap, 23

Sanders, Barry, 5, 6-7, 11, 28-29, 31, 37
Sanders, Charlie, 39
Sanders, "Neon" Deion, 42
Sayers, Gale, 5, 25-26, 28, 34, 43
Simpson, O.J., 5, 19, 23, 26-27, 28, 31, 33
    34, 37
Smith, Emmitt, 15
special teams, 40-43
Stagg, Amos Alonzo, 7-8
Strong, Ken, 33

Taylor, Jim, 14
Thomas, Thurman, 11, 29
Thorpe, Jim, 4, 5, 8-9, 13, 31, 34
Thurston, Fuzzy, 20
tight ends, 38-40

Warren, Don, 39
Williams, John L., 37
Williams, Travis, 43

Younger, Paul, 33